Key Stage 2
Science
Assessment Papers

for the
National Curriculum

5

Name _____

Class _____

1. Work carefully.
2. Ask your teacher if there is something you do not understand.

Schofield & Sims

Today's date:

1

Here are four living things. They look very different.

In some ways they are all the same: they all need food and they all reproduce.

Write down three other things that they all do.

1 _____

2 _____

3 _____

2

Josie has been running in the playground. She is breathing quickly.

a) Why do you think Josie has to breathe quickly when she runs? Write your answer here.

_____
_____
_____
_____

b) Before Josie starts running, her pulse rate is quite slow. What happens to her pulse rate while she is running?

_____

c) What happens to her pulse rate about five minutes after she stops running?

_____

A.T.2 – Life Processes and Living Things

Life processes
Humans as organisms

Level 5

3 Describe what these parts of the flower do:

The stamen _____
_____

The stigma _____
_____

The petals _____
_____

4 Leaves make food for plants in a process called **photosynthesis**.
This is a diagram of photosynthesis.

a) Name the two substances needed for photosynthesis.
_____

b) Where does the energy come from for photosynthesis?
_____

c) Name the food made by photosynthesis.
_____

d) Write down two reasons why photosynthesis is important to living things. _____
_____
_____

A.T.2 – Life Processes and Living Things — Green plants as organisms

5

Which animals are described here?

**Choose names from the box to match the descriptions.
But take care! There are more animal names than descriptions.**

| earthworm | jellyfish | frog | alligator |
| dolphin | eagle | fruit bat | salmon |

Animal A has a backbone, breathes with lungs, has scales all over its body, lays eggs, is cold-blooded. It lives mostly in water, but comes onto land.

It is _____

Animal B has warm blood, lives in water, has no hair, has lungs and its young are born alive.

It is _____

Animal C has a mouth surrounded by tentacles and no backbone.

It is _____

Animal D has a long, round body with segments and no backbone.

It is _____

Animal E has a backbone, breathes with gills, has scales all over its body, lays eggs and is cold-blooded.

It is _____

Animal F has fur, breathes with lungs, is warm-blooded, has two wings and two legs.

It is _____

A.T.2 – Life Processes and Living Things   Variation and classification

Level 5

6 Ricky was looking under some stones near the school pond. He found some earthworms, wood lice and slugs.

Write three reasons why these animals live under a stone.

a) _____

b) _____

c) _____

7 Ali and Tom wanted to find a way to stop food going mouldy. They put four slices of bread in different conditions and saw what happened.

Slice 1 Dried in an oven, sealed in a plastic bag and put in the dark. No mould after 3 weeks.

Slice 2 Sealed in plastic bag and placed in the fridge. Mouldy after one week.

Slice 3 Sealed in plastic bag and left in the freezer. No mould after 3 weeks.

Slice 4 Sealed in plastic bag and put in a dark place. Mouldy after four days.

a) Write down two ways that Ali and Tom found to stop the bread going mouldy.

1 _____

2 _____

b) Why is it important to cover food when it is being stored?

_____

_____

A.T.2 – Life Processes and Living Things — Living things in their environment

Today's date:

8

Sara was watching a pond. She saw a frog eat a caterpillar. She saw a heron eat a frog. She saw a caterpillar eat a leaf.

a) Arrange this information into a food chain.

| leaf | → | | → | | → | |

b) Choose words from the box to complete the sentences correctly.

herbivores   carnivores   omnivores   predators   producers

1 Caterpillars only eat plants.

They are called _____ .

2 Herons look for small creatures to eat and kill them.

They are called _____ .

3 Frogs and herons are both called _____

because they survive by eating other animals.

4 Leaves get their energy from the Sun.

Leaves are called _____ .

A.T.2 – Life Processes and Living Things   Living things in their environment

Level 5

9 Which gas is produced when you burn a candle?

Tick ✓ the correct box.

hydrogen ☐   air ☐   oxygen ☐

carbon dioxide ☐   nitrogen ☐

10 Julie and Sofia were going on a school trip. They wanted to keep their soup hot. They carried out an experiment to help them decide the best way to do this.

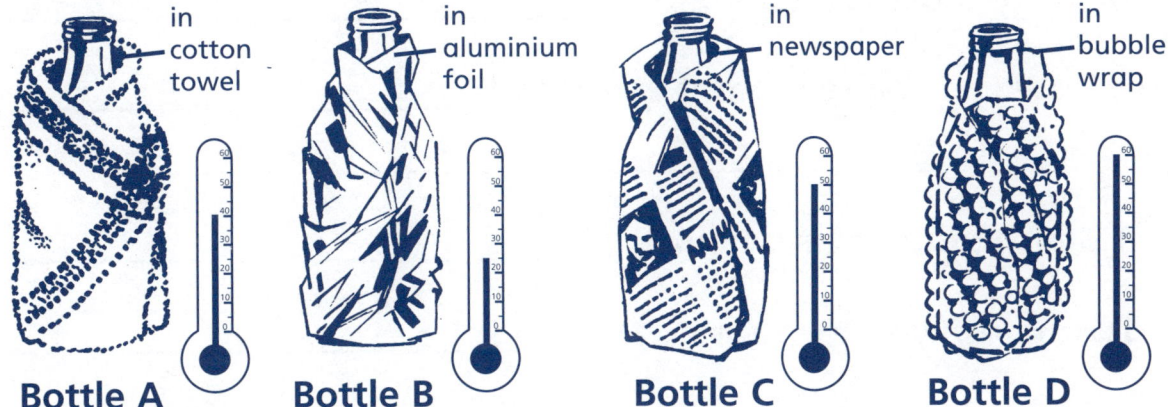

Bottle A — in cotton towel
Bottle B — in aluminium foil
Bottle C — in newspaper
Bottle D — in bubble wrap

They filled each bottle with water at 70° Celsius. After one hour, they checked the temperature of each one with a thermometer.

a) Read the thermometers and write down the temperatures on the chart below.

	Temperature after one hour
Bottle A	
Bottle B	
Bottle C	
Bottle D	

b) Which material do you think they should choose to wrap around their soup bottle? _____

c) Why should they choose that material? _____
_____

A.T.3 – Materials and Their Properties   Grouping and classifying materials   7

Today's date:

11

Imagine that three materials have just been discovered called avlon, brodium and crogine.

Read this information about them and use the information to answer the questions.

> Avlon and crogine feel hard when you touch them. Brodium boils when you heat it. Avlon can be bent into different shapes and it is attracted towards a magnet. Lumps of crogine can be crushed to form a powder.

a) Which material is a metal? _____

b) How can you tell that it is a metal? _____
_____

c) Which material is a liquid? _____

d) How can you tell that it is a liquid? _____

e) Can you think of one other property that avlon might have?
_____

12

a) Gardeners use wire coated in plastic to tie up plants in the garden .

Why do you think they use this sort of wire?
_____

b) Fuse wire is used to mend fuses.
Fuse wire is not coated in plastic.

Why do you think fuse wire is not coated in plastic?
_____
_____

A.T.3 – Materials and Their Properties   Grouping and classifying materials
Changing materials

13

a) Look at this picture.

Why are there drops of water on the inside of the window?
_____

b) Why is ice hanging from the outside water tap?
_____

14 This garage sells several different fuels.

a) Write down the names of:

One solid fuel _____

Two liquid fuels _____

One gas fuel _____

b) Choose the words from this list to complete the sentences.

| oxygen | water | burns |
| carbon dioxide | combustion | energy |

A fuel is a substance that _____ . When it burns it releases _____ . When a fuel burns it uses up _____ and it produces _____ and _____ . Another word for burning is _____ .

A.T.3 – Materials and Their Properties Changing materials

Today's date:

15 How can these mixtures be separated?

Draw a line to join each mixture to the process that is used to separate the substances in it.

Mixtures	Process
Oil and water	Chromatography
Salt and water	Filtration
Red ink and blue ink	Distillation
Sand and water	Evaporation

16 Mary added salt to a beaker of water until no more salt would dissolve in the water.

a) How can she get the salt back out of the water?

_____

_____

b) How can she get back pure water?

_____

_____

_____

A.T.3 – Materials and Their Properties   Separating mixtures of materials

Level 5

17 Anwar is investigating the colours in five felt-tipped pens. He has five strips of filter paper and makes a mark with a different pen near the bottom of each strip. Then he stands the paper in water. The paper soaks up the water and looks like this:

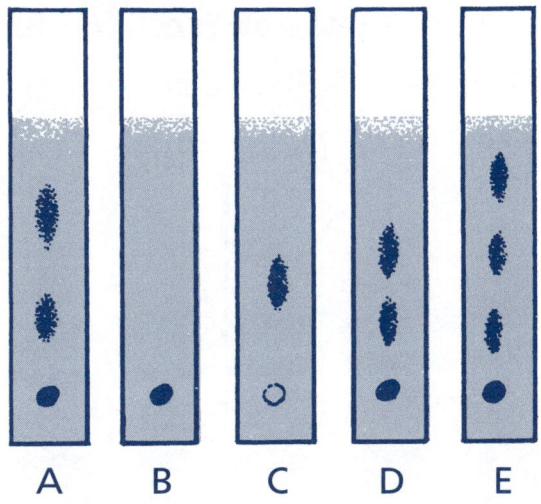

a) Which ink is a pure substance? _____

b) Which ink contains the most colours? _____

c) Which ink is from a permanent marker pen? _____

d) How can you tell which ink is from the permanent marker?

_____

_____

18 This diagram shows how drinking water can be obtained in the desert.

Choose the best words from this list to complete the sentences below. You will not need to use all the words.

| boils   vapour   cold   condenses   distils   hot   evaporates |

Water in the hot sand _____ and forms water _____ in the hole. At night, when the air is _____, the water vapour _____ on the plastic sheet and drips into the cup.

A.T.3 – Materials and Their Properties   Separating mixtures of materials   11

19 Hannah connected a cell, a bulb and a variable resistor to make this circuit.

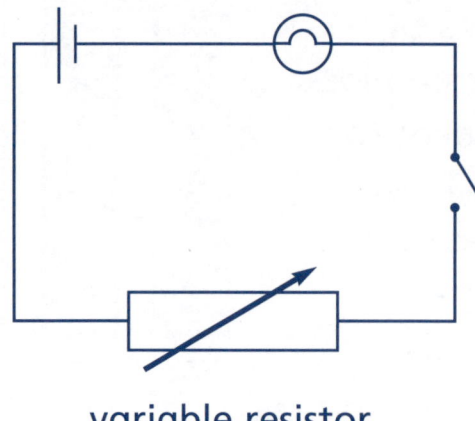

variable resistor

a) She adjusted the variable resistor to make the bulb dimmer.

What effect does this have on the current in the circuit?

_____

b) Hannah added two further cells to her circuit.

Draw a diagram below to show her new circuit.

c) What effect do the two extra cells have on the current in the circuit?

_____

d) What do the two new cells do to the brightness of the bulb?

_____

A.T.4 – Physical Processes

Electricity

Level 5

20 Joe has made a model traffic light.

The circuit diagram looks like this.

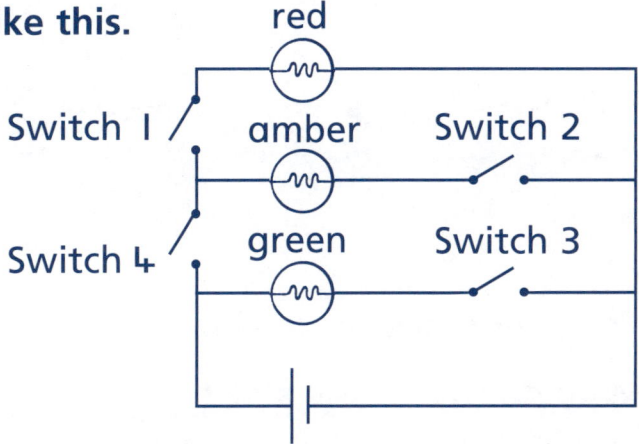

a) Which bulbs light when Joe closes the following switches?

Switch 1 _____

Switch 3 _____

Switches 1 and 4 _____

b) Which switches must Joe close to make the red and amber bulbs light at the same time? _____

21 This plane is flying through the air.

There are four forces acting on it, labelled A, B, C and D.

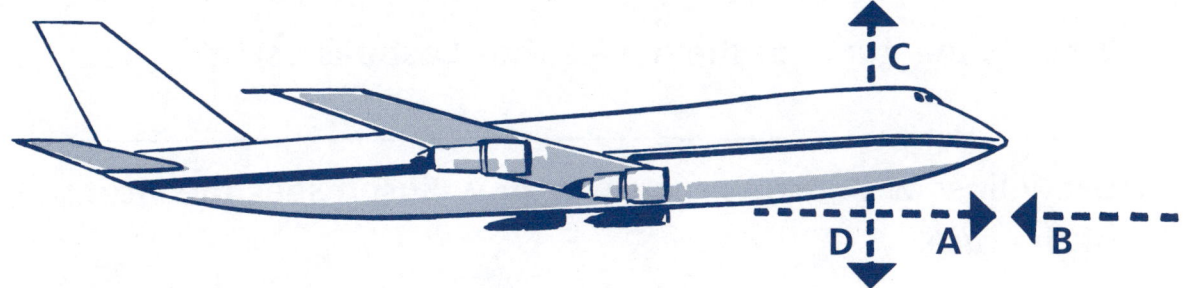

a) Which arrow represents gravity? _____

b) Which arrow represents air resistance? _____

c) What force does arrow C represent? _____

d) Which arrow represents the driving force? _____

A.T.4 – Physical Processes

Electricity
Forces and motion

Today's date:

22

Jessie is floating in the swimming pool.

weight force

upthrust force

a) Draw two arrows to show the two forces acting on her body.

b) Why doesn't Jessie sink? _____

_____

_____

23

Sasha is watching a sprint race. He has made a device to help him see over the crowd.

mirror

mirror

a) What is the name of the device that Sasha is using?

_____

b) Draw lines with arrows to show how Sasha sees the start of the race.

c) Sasha sees the smoke from the starter's gun before he hears the 'bang'. Why is this? _____

_____

_____

_____

14 A.T.4 – Physical Processes

Forces and motion
Light and sound

Level 5

24 This is a simple musical instrument. It has four strings. They are all made of the same material. Each string has a mass tied to it.

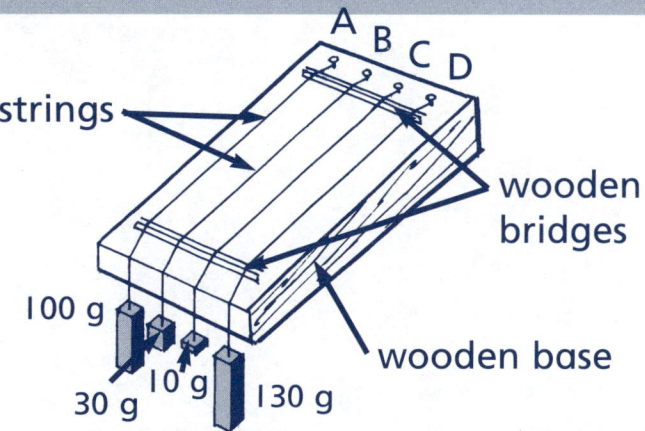

a) How can you produce sounds with this instrument?
_____

b) Which string will give the highest note?_____

c) If all the masses were the same, how could you produce different notes? _____
_____

25 a) Draw a line to show the movement of the Moon during one month.

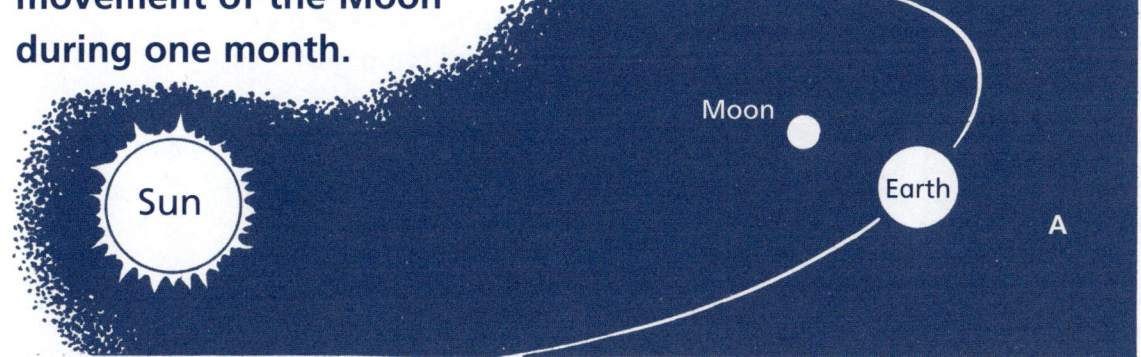

b) How long does it take the Moon to reach point A?
_____

c) If you lived at point B, what would you notice about the number of hours of daylight in each day as the Earth orbits the Sun?

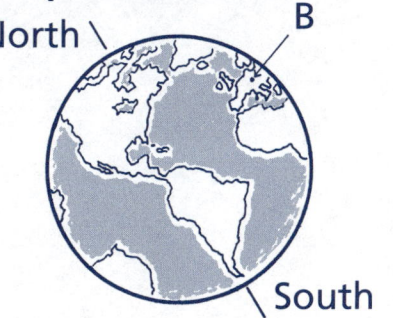

_____
_____

A.T.4 – Physical Processes
Light and sound
The Earth and beyond

These papers are based on the Programmes of Study in **Science** at **Key Stage 2**. They provide a wide variety of assessment opportunities in Science skills, knowledge and understanding.

They are designed as an aid to the teacher's judgement when assessing a child's progress and deciding on levels of achievement. Therefore they should be used within the context of the teacher's knowledge of individual children.

They are not prescriptive in determining levels, but offer valuable indicators to depth and width of ability. Nor are they intended to be sole markers of attainment at any level and it is not anticipated that every child will succeed in every exercise offered in the different skills before being awarded a particular level.

They are a useful aid in planning and in work preparation and differentiation. They also provide a valuable record of progress when informing colleagues or reporting to parents.

Teachers should give help and explanation to children who do not understand initial instructions. Spare paper should be provided for any working out.

© 1997 Schofield & Sims Ltd.

All rights reserved. No reproduction, copy or transmission of this publication may be made without written permission.

No paragraph of this publication may be reproduced, copied or transmitted, save with written copyright permission or in accordance with the Copyright Act 1956 (as amended).

Any person who does any unauthorised act in relation to this publication may be liable to criminal prosecution and civil claims for damages.

First printed 1997.

This is one of **four levels** of Science Assessment Papers for Key Stage 2.

Level 2
ASSESSMENT PAPERS	0 7217 3609 2
ANSWERS	0 7217 3613 0

Level 3
ASSESSMENT PAPERS	0 7217 3610 6
ANSWERS	0 7217 3614 9

Level 4
ASSESSMENT PAPERS	0 7217 3611 4
ANSWERS	0 7217 3615 7

Level 5
ASSESSMENT PAPERS	0 7217 3612 2
ANSWERS	0 7217 3616 5

Life processes
Humans as organisms
Green plants as organisms
Variation and classification
Living things in their environment
Grouping and classifying materials
Separating mixtures of materials
Changing materials
Electricity
Forces and motion
Light and sound
The Earth and beyond

Warning
These publications are *not* part of the copyright licensing scheme run by the Copyright Licensing Agency and may not be photocopied or mechanically copied in any other way, without permission from the publisher.

Design and typesetting by Armitage Typo/Graphics
Printed by Hawthornes, Nottingham

Schofield & Sims Ltd, Huddersfield

ISBN 0-7217-3612-2